Figures of Dead Men
by Leonard Baskin

Figures of Dead Men
by Leonard Baskin

PREFACE BY ARCHIBALD MACLEISH

PHOTOGRAPHS BY HYMAN EDELSTEIN

THE UNIVERSITY OF MASSACHUSETTS PRESS 1968

"LEONARD BASKIN," says the critic, "an artist preoccupied with death." Or is it life?

One can understand the statement. Baskin produced in the nineteen-fifties a series of figures of dead men made to lie on a floor or on the ground, some with hands and feet, some without, some with two arms, some with one or none.

These dead men, moreover, were not dead by designation only: they were truly dead—more truly dead than their predecessors in the history of art, the dead Christs, the lords and ladies of the mediaeval sarcophagi, the cocoons of cotton which contain the eviscerated Pharaohs of the Egyptian embalmers. The dead Christs are not dead: they have conquered death—they have the Third Day before them. The mediaeval lords and ladies are not dead: they are waiting— asleep and waiting on their marble pallets in the shuffling silence of the vast cathedrals. It is because they are asleep and waiting that the cathedrals are so still, the motes in the shafts of sunlight so miraculously suspended, the shuffling tourists so bored and unconcerned. Death leaves no one unconcerned: it collects crowds around the stoops of the humblest houses when the wooden box is carried out, attracts multitudes from the remotest continents to the pits of mingled bones in Germany and Poland. And as for the Pharaoh in his intricate wrappings he is the least dead of all. He is on a journey. He has the necessities of his journey around him: his food, his gold, his ship. It is because he is on a journey that he is exhibited not in a temple or burial place but in a museum. Those who come to the museum do not see his death: they see his journey. It is true they do not believe in his journey but they see it: they do not see his death.

But with Baskin's dead men it is different. They are dead. They are not asleep, they are not on a journey, they are not waiting for a trumpet or for the removal of a stone or the visitation of an angel: they are dead. Their mouths are dead, their flaccid bowels are dead, their pudenda are dead, their bones under their flesh are dead men's bones. The Great Dead Man of 1961 is wrapped in his grave clothes as a mummy in his mummy cloth, but The Great Dead Man is not a mummy, a traveller to eternity, a seed in a husk. He is dead: truly and unalterably dead. As is the armless, footless dead man of 1952. And the fat dead man of 1954. And all the rest of them.

So that one can understand very well why the critic says: "Leonard Baskin, an artist preoccupied with death." But why it is said and whether or not it is true are different questions. It is not true.

What does it mean to be preoccupied with death? Was the Christian preoccupied with death who postponed his life until his death, who spent his days in the contemplation of his death: the Saint who slept in his grave clothes in his own tomb? Is the decadent philosopher preoccupied with death who so surrenders himself to the horror of dying that his dread extinguishes not only the love of life but the meaning of life leaving nothing but the absurdity of existing in a world in which men die? But if these are preoccupied with death what shall we say of the man who neither fears death nor loves it but can look at it?

And how, in any case, is an artist preoccupied with death? By making images of death? Baudelaire in *Une Charogne* makes an image of death so compelling that no one who has read the poem can ever again be free of it. And yet Cézanne, to his life's end, went back and back to that image as to the bread of his life and of his art. For what is compelling in this carrion of Baudelaire is not the horror of the putrescence but the likeness to something else.

Les jambes en l'air, comme une femme lubrique . . .
Here, for Cézanne and for many others, that *analogie universelle* which is the key to art and therefore the key to life is made visible.

No, it is not the making of images of death which enlists an artist in the cause of death but the use of those images. If they are employed as certain contemporary writers and artists employ them to belittle life or to demean life they serve death. If they are used as Baudelaire uses them in *Une Charogne* they enhance life and their loyalty is to life.

As Leonard Baskin's is. Consider how these dead men of his are used. First, to show death. Which means to show death itself: not sleeping death or waiting death or journeying death but death—men dead. This they do: they *show death.*

Second, to show not only death but a particular death, a death we can recognize, our own death. This also they succeed in showing. They are men like ourselves with bodies like ours, slack and sedentary, and faces, gross and Roman, like our own.

But showing death, and showing also our own death, they show something more, something which is not of death but life, our own life. They show us that our life has changed by showing that our death has changed. For thousands of years we died wakening deaths and waiting deaths because the misery and suffering and bestiality of our lives was such that only by restitution elsewhere could they be borne. Now we die death. Which means we are no longer willing to wait for restitution elsewhere. Which means we no longer accept the misery and the suffering and the bestiality. Which means that we are determined, whether or not our determination is declared, to change the world and to know what is necessary for us to know and to live in this place and die in it.

It is for this reason that Baskin's dead men, slack and unheroic as they are, are heavy with grandeur. It is the grandeur of their mortality. And it is for this reason that they are alien among those earlier dead. Imagine them upon the pavement of the crypt of Chartres!

ARCHIBALD MACLEISH

Conway, Massachusetts

Figures of Dead Men
by Leonard Baskin

[1952 a]

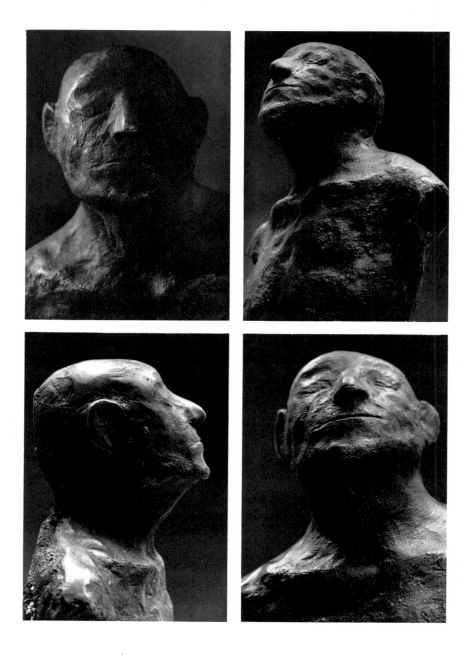

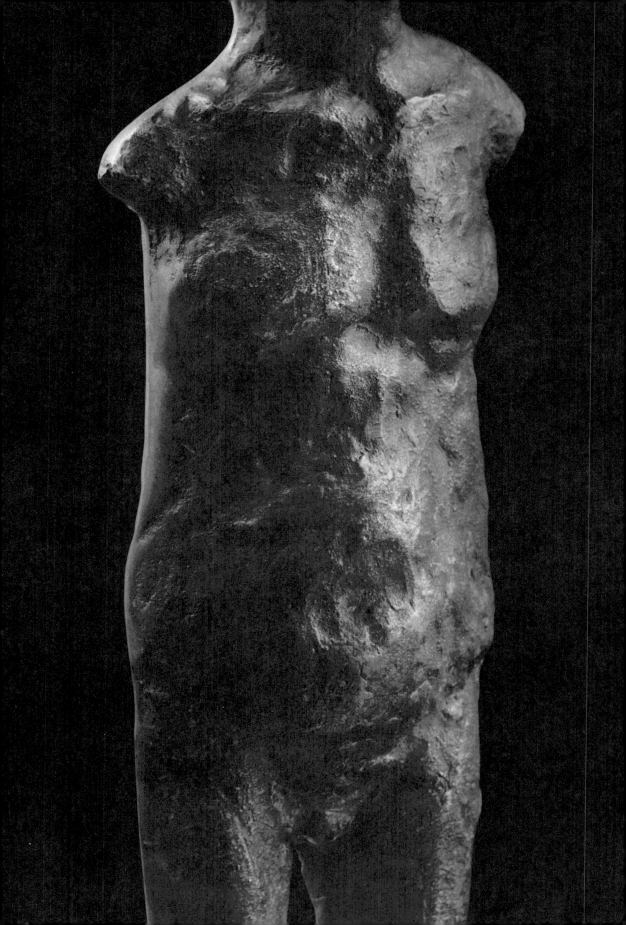

[1952 b]

$\left[1952 \ c \right]$

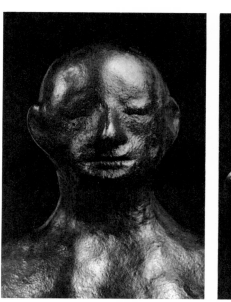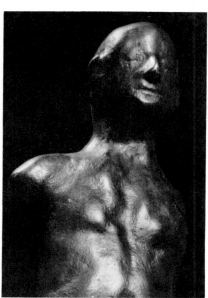

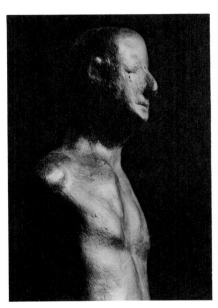 

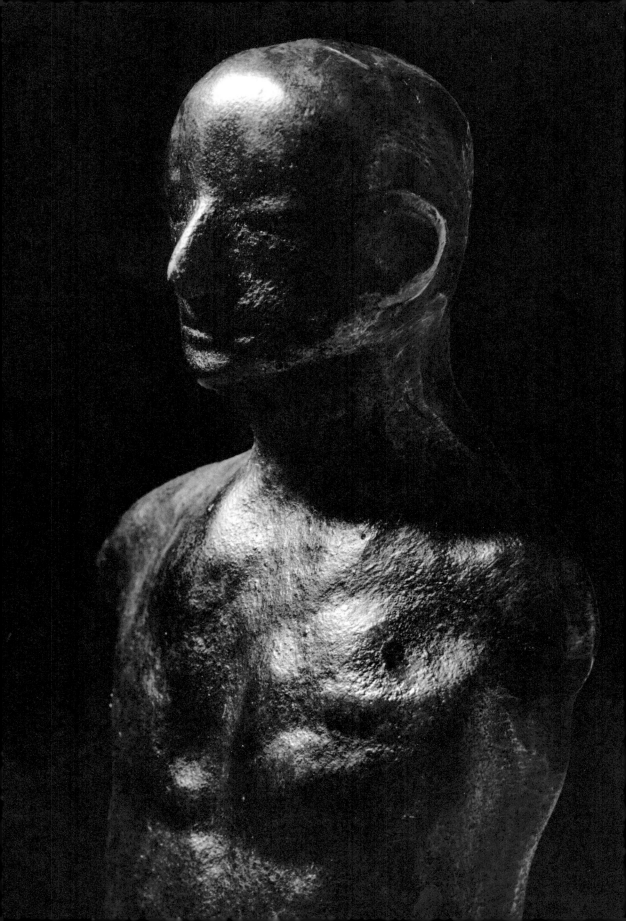

$\left[\text{1955 a}\right]$

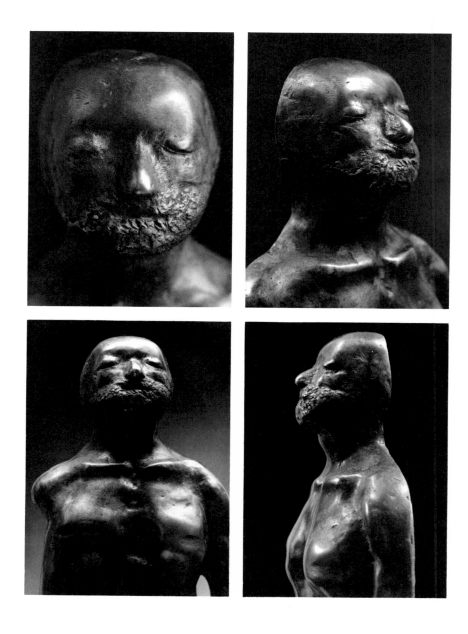

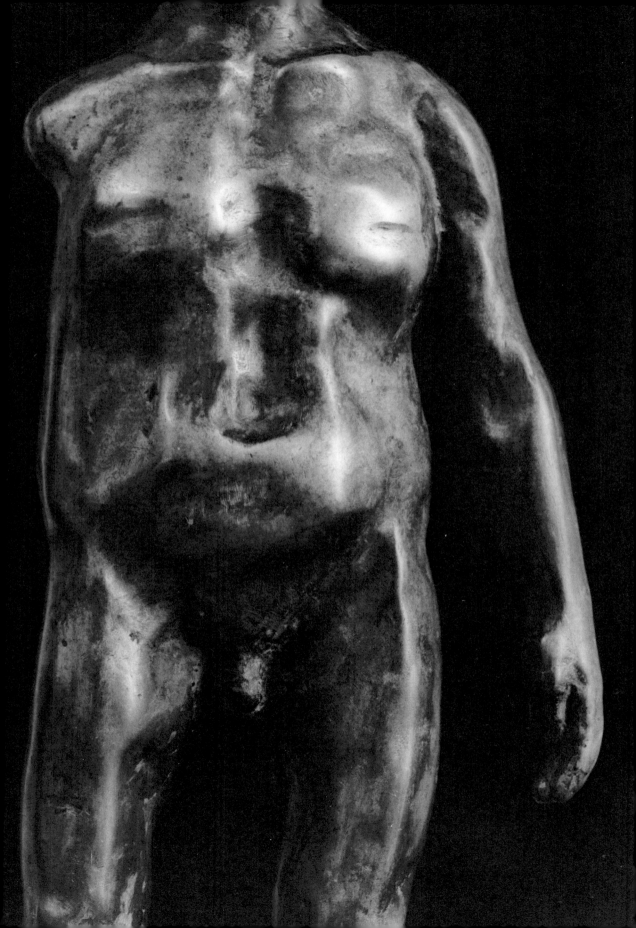

[1955 b]

[1955 c]

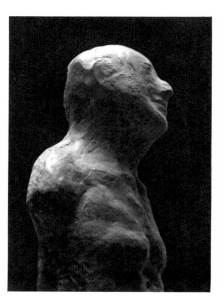 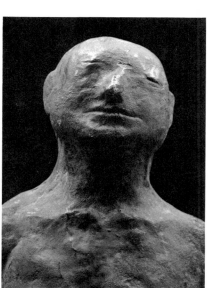

[1956]
Great Stone Dead Man

PHOTOGRAPH BY PAUL KRAUSE

[1956 a]

[1956 b]

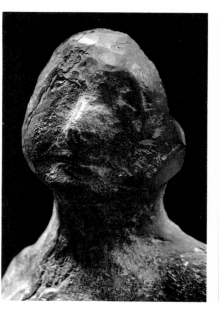

[1956 c]

PHOTOGRAPH BY PAUL KRAUSE

[1961]
Great Bronze Dead Man

[1966]

[1967 a]

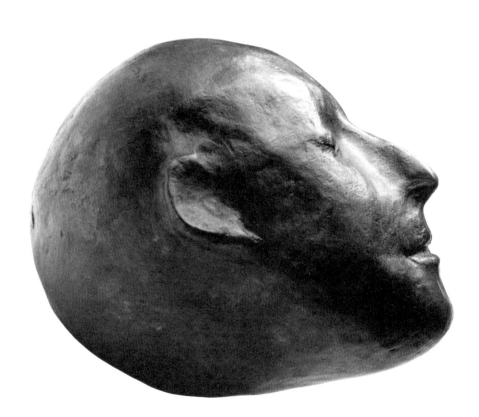

[1967 b]

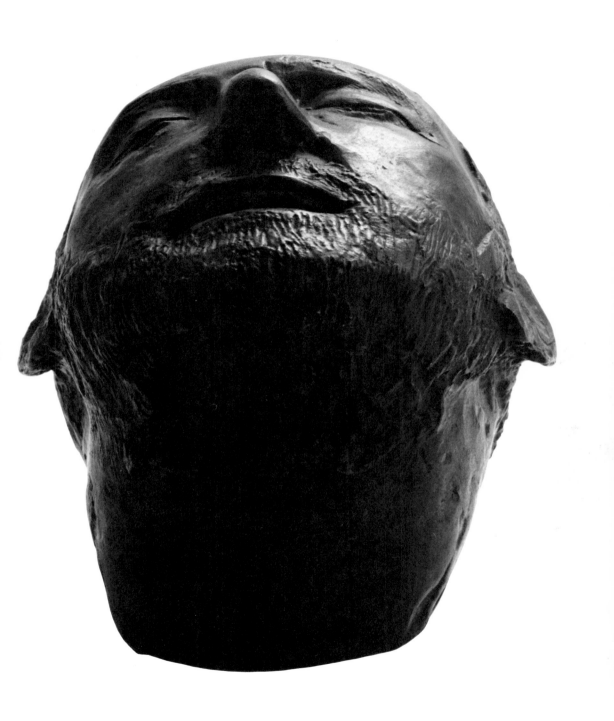

[1968]
Great Wood Dead Man

LIST OF FIGURES

[1961]
Great Bronze Dead Man
Bronze. 84 inches

[1966]
Bronze. 30 inches

[1967a]
Bronze. 4 inches

[1967b]
Bronze. Life size

[1968]
Great Wood Dead Man
Walnut. 68½ inches
WORK IN PROGRESS